Give Me a Fragment
Glimpses into Motherhood, Depression, and Hope

by Cheryl Seely Savage

Give Me a Fragment

Copyright © 2019 by Cheryl Seely Savage

All rights reserved.

First paperback edition February 2019

Book design using Canva by the author

ISBN 9781796764697 (paperback)

Dedication

*For Laurzia
who told me this is what I should be writing.*

TABLE OF CONTENTS:

Although the poems have been divided into three categories, most themes flow between them. The theme of hope (often hope in God) is found in almost everything I write, especially in the poems about mental illness. The beautiful part about poetry is how several themes can be found within the words of a single poem; the layers exist, whether or not they are intentional.

Please notice the category Marriage. *I didn't include this in the title of this book, as the bulk of my poetry deals with my Depression and Motherhood. However, it needs to be explained that my marriage has offered a lot of hope. My husband has been a faithful partner and friend for more than twenty years, and his care for me has provided invaluable support. Without him, I believe Depression could have claimed me many years ago.*

MENTAL ILLNESS 1

    FRAGMENTS 3
    COMING HOME 4
    MORTALITY 5
    INSECURITY 7
    CHANGE 9
    OVERCOMPENSATION 11
    I DON'T KNOW 12
    MIST 13
    FLOWERS ON MY TABLE 14
    I CAN'T SEEM TO STOP TALKING 15
    COMPLIMENTS 16
    FORGIVENESS 17
    MOMENTS OF CHOICE 19
    ASTHMA 22

MOTHERHOOD 23

    SECOND ESTATE 25
    SENSES 26
    MOTHER OF MANY 27
    IRREPLACEABLE 28
    BROKEN HEART 29

MARRIAGE 30
- Marriage 32
- Refocus 33
- Love Stories 34
- I Breathe, I Joy 36

ABOUT THE AUTHOR 37

Mental Illness

Give Me a Fragment

Fragments

(2007)

Fleeting it seems, this
Happiness
Which comes not once,
But as shards, piercing through this blanket of sorrow.
Gathering, glimmering,
Hoping, helping;
Reflecting Another's increasing triumph over covers
Which muffle the voice of truth.
Give me a fragment,
One by one.
If carefully,
It will be enough.

Coming Home

(2019)

The darkness is not sad, you see,
It is devoid of hope

And when you step down inside,
It is easy to forget how you got there

Because you cannot see the door

Even as you grope for it blindly
While the darkness pulls you deeper

Until you let it turn you around
And lose your footing on purpose

Because it is comfortable.

Mortality

(2009)

And there I went.
Over rays and Under waves
Crashing, coursing, chafing, cursing,
Marking time with leaf patterns; searching
Veins of plant-life
Wondering, Wandering
Chasing distorted light.

Unsure-hesitant I stood
Naked before myself.
Exposed the soul-spirit, I
Drank, Gulped, Devoured the Truth above me.
"I am light and before me is
Color.
I am worth and behind me is
Black-grey.
I am strength and beside me are
Lifted wings."

Warrior on!
Keep in stance and
Stay in currents fresh from
Wildflowers, pure with snow,
Smelling of morning and oak.
In them I let go,
Escape from shackled exhaustion,
Tethered standards, faceless tradition
and find Joy;
unfettered, unresolved, pointless.
Happiness freckled with turbulence, yet
Resounded in liberty!

Priceless freedom to feel.

Insecurity

(2017)

Dried out, that's how I feel
Consuming exhaustion that doesn't happen because I don't get
enough sleep;
I get plenty of sleep
But I don't get to rest from worry and frustration
from wondering constantly if I will ever be
good enough.

Good enough for what? Excellent question
that can't be answered with trite or cliche
and instead burrows even deeper into my mind and comes
out to play when I need it to disappear the most.

Vulnerable rejection based on mistakes in my behavior
but not in my character
Except --what makes a character if not the behavior?

I rely too much on the outside when I should be
illuminating from the inside
and attempting not to change my environment or the people
around me
but my own awkward perceptions
found deep in the bottom parts of my soul.

Give Me a Fragment

It's a cavern full of dried up, masticated doubt
and every single time I get to the place where I
think, this! I am finally rid of that annoying
insecurity!
It leaps up from the shadows and
burns
my
very
Flesh.

Change

(2012)

Slowly drifting far away
within the wood of bonded clay
breaking bands with public light
which skews amongst the cabin's fright

"take me on (I want to stay?)
it won't be long before I say
that moving forward, back to sea
was simply where I had to be."

but gales of wind keep me back,
those gusts of mourning, breezes black.
which is right, the sea or shore?
taking less or giving more?

it does not speak, the matter's done
the boat has launched, the deed is sung

within the moaning sound of pain
a whisper shouts its last refrain
reminds me how the tethered land
stole myself, abhorred my stand.

Give Me a Fragment

turn about, forget the past
hoist the sail upon the mast
fight the wind of black delight
forward, forward, canvas white!

the crumbling earth left far behind
was not foundation, how did it bind
my heart to man, to mocking scorn
blowing forth the tempter's horn?

storms or calm within the sea
each will give my heart to Thee
those who thrust my boat from shore
only made my heart give more.

thirsty raindrops wash my face;
tears announce His sweet embrace.

Overcompensation

(2017)

I over-watered the orchid.

It drowned in a pool of soil and hydrogen and oxygen,

petals falling one by one

as the stem withered, gasping for breath

and I feel horrible.

I Don't Know

(2012)

Who I was and who I am cross paths
In the road, like a motorist, who
Texting or talking or reaching for something
Hits a deer, and everything is metal
And massive tragedy.

I make alliances with the new system
And then it changes, like a rug --
Oriental and expensive, charged with
Static, pulled, violently from underneath
Leaving me charred.

I claim it doesn't matter, that I can
Adjust, like sails on a ship; the mainsheet
Shifting canvas with ease. Only I forget
That manpower is needed to thread
Ropes through pulleys.

I go on pretending unaffection, hiding in
Coldness, like drafts sweeping through
An old house, the heater broken and
Lying in twisted heaps next to
Rotting wooden beams.

I am tossed about and taken without
Warning, like an apple dropped into a
Vast river, flowing, crashing, out to Sea
Where birds, desperate for sustenance
Eat what they find.

Mist

(2008)

As mist they come, these days taken in
Pieces, not given in hours but
Moments defined by singular fascination.
Drifting; muted, matted, music of such
Loud silence it treads the
Skin and melts into careful formulations.
Even when vanished by
Pointed light, such melody lingers to
Speak of dew and damp, cool and crisp,
Freshness which fills the lungs and awakens
Sadness to look upward, not down,
Forward, not back.
So I wait for mist and watch for
Dew, hoping not once, but thrice these
Moments will appear before
Dawn carries them from outreached
Fingers. Stay near me, moments of
Mist; give me such
Happiness.

Flowers on My Table

(2016)

Hazy light filters into the room through panes of chipped wood
And the flowers on my table are changing color.

Once red, brown seeps in; once white, yellow creeps out of folded petals.
Former glory is replaced with drooping, depressed heads;
Buds that never fulfilled their purpose before succumbing
To the impatient obsession of my own hand.

Desiring their beauty, I cut them, pretending I have not killed them.
In my pitcher I pour water, dashes of sugar, and plunge the green shards into a
Temporary suspension of time.

But none can slow decay,
So the flowers begin to wilt, even before my eyes.
I never notice until I look away for far too long, and then
Sincerely, stupidly, stunningly surprised I turn back and illuminated by the sunrise,
I see the death before me.

I Can't Seem to Stop Talking

(2019)

It is difficult to speak
When words have been chastised
And a heart needs bold understanding.

But despite all the bruising
My tongue isn't silenced;
Continues to sing out unyielding

The feelings, all cerebral,
Not filtered (nor focused)
Carefully laid out for postponing

Inevitable judgment.
It comes, the rejection
Simply hurtful, yet not surprising.

Compliments

(2019)

I deflect the compliments when they come
Because I am a realist and if they saw, if they knew...

If they knew what? That I am flawed?
Everyone is flawed and most people are
Really gross.

There isn't anything within me that could
Surprise because we are all the same.

I have never met a perfect person and the
One person who is perfect would
Compliment me.

Forgiveness

(2016)

I hear the words she is speaking, but I can see her words are only partly true.
Her eyes, her hands --they betray her thoughts, and even though she speaks sweetly, with
Honey and roses, I can feel the partial lie of them even before the vibrations touch my ears.

She means well, she hopes well, she longs for forgiveness,
Even if she cannot give me truth or sincerity in this well-planned, shower-practiced
Barrage of words which pour over me like water that is not quite ready to bathe in.

I have an immediate choice, and in moments, I struggle with indecision.
Forgiveness means letting it go.
Forgiveness means passing by the bitterness.
Forgiveness means refusing to pick up the grudge that is present in her hands...

I stare at her eyes, guarding my secret knowledge and wondering what she would do,
If only she knew how well I could read her intentions and weakness.

I decide, only once, and it is enough, as my arms
Wrap around her, releasing the grudge, releasing the bitter, releasing her weakness --
Releasing my own --
But...
Trust is not part of the package, and as I release even her and stare into her face,
I know we will never again be the same.

Moments of Choice

(2015)

These moments are ones I cherish. Without irony or
Abuse of the word;
The ones where the house smells of apple
And is vacuumed.

All of the children are home and I am in the
Kitchen, cooking dinner, hearing:
Laughter from outside,
Tutoring math problems upstairs,
Baby giggles,
Peace.

The separation between Depression and Light
Is only found in these tiny moments of
Choice --
Decision --
The power of Agency, which seem so simple and
Yet,
Those dark weights blur the lines until I am only capable
To wonder:

Do I care about this; do I want to?

I can't move, I can't decide, I can't wonder, I can't decide. I can't, I can't... I can't...

But here, today, in this kitchen, with the scent of apples, the sight of roses, the laughter of children, the dishes washed, the meal cooking,

I want it. I chose it.

I choose it.

And the darkness lingers, but it has no power, because the
Power of My Agency
Has a fire-light, and it is burning brightly!
Taller and stronger than those weights,
Those fingers,
Those arms of oppression and slavery.

Each time I add fuel (medical, inspirational, Grace,
And oh! How Great is His Grace!), I feel the
Heat grow.
One blade of grass here... another blade there...
Blades of moments gathered as harvest from the
Spirit of my soul -- dried out from pain, dried out from
Desperate hope.

The drying hurts,
But the drying fuels.

This darkness, this pain, this exhausting weight is
Losing
Because every time it dries me out, every time it pulls away my
Choices, it doesn't realize --
Just as serpents in Gardens where arrogance cannot understand (and did
They not realize?) --
Each dried blade brings me to

Him

And fuels the very Fire that will set me
Free.

Asthma

(2019)

You cannot tell me how it feels
Because I have already felt all of it
Here, deep, right there; in my lungs

I gasped.

I've breathed in every rejection, every betrayal
They smelled of perfumed sheets
And ammonia-filled toilet cleaner and

It burned.

From the inside out, it still burns, even though
I shower and sing and blow balloons
It sticks inside the lining of my bronchioles

And aches.

Motherhood

Second Estate

(2007)

Sweet agony! Oh, sweating pain! The Door by
Which enters Breath, soft Breath, and fills the room with quiet relief.

Agony gone and pain suppressed,
Perfection embodied and counting, one, two, three, four, five...
Each hand embarking, not knowing, having chosen

With Love in the left, and
Faith in the right,
Each curled up in safety,
Tightly, tightly.
Mother, than father hold
Tightly, tightly.

Love and Faith
Bounded, bonded, begins.

Senses

(2016)

How did it come to be that the inhalation and vibrations of air (the
Reflection of light!) could cause
Such ecstatic electricity inside of a mind,
With pulsing, pounding,
Soothing, sounding,
Constant rush of emotion through veins that are
Wired for nothing more than carrying oxygen to
Organs that cannot logically,
Nor justifiably, (perhaps scientifically?)
Feel the poignant and exhilarating rush of
Memory?

Mother of Many

(2019)

I cannot decide if I am
Refracted light or broken pieces

Either way, I am divided,
Forced in myriads of directions

Pulled to this and prodded backward
I go willingly and thoughtfully

But I never quite find comfort
In knowing how much I am needed

By those who forget so quickly,
Although not even maliciously,

To say thank you.

Irreplaceable

(2019)

Lists are long and include tasks such as:
Cat feeding, child feeding, husband feeding,
Soul feeding
And don't forget to
Wash, rinse (repeat)
Fold, place, find, create
There won't be time to also
Serve, donate, care, sweep
Maybe bake
And
Vitamins, running, parent-teacher-conferences
Followed with the brushing of teeth
And holding together all the dreams, hygiene,
Tangible items, schedules, tidying, and potential
For an entire family
Without
Falling
Apart.
I'm basically glue.

Broken Heart

(2016)

The pieces of my heart are not found
Among blood vessels and tissue
Nor muscle, housed in bone.

They are soft shards,
Wandering about in places both
In and out of my soul.

Each has been created out of love,
Grown through pain,
And forever defined in joy.

Even though my heart beats on,
It misses each piece
As they pull away from me.

I will not fault them;
They were meant for greater things
Than the cavity of my chest.

But there will always be a space
Inside of me
Waiting for their return

Should they ever need to
Find the place of
Their beginning, again.

Marriage

Marriage

(2016)

It is more than a dance, this thing between us.
We are learning and growing simultaneously
But never exactly in sync.

Our passion is subtle because it is deep.
From romantic longings, our shared movement has
Risen from frost and ash.

Our goal of enduring love has never changed.
How we attempt to arrive continuously changes as the
Sand beneath us shifts.

Fear has tried to destroy our awkward clinging.
But loyalty sparks love, and forgiveness claims us as
We clumsily adjust our footing.

Refocus

(2017)

It is an easy thing to overlook true love.
Our eyes are searching for events and objects
Found in movies,
Novels,
And journals bursting with dreams.

We glance above the murky reality.
Our hearts do not notice the consistent presence
Of loyalty,
Friendship,
And dishes again scrubbed clean.

Love Stories

(2019)

Jane told me, in writing (six times!),
How misunderstandings make eloquent
Love stories.

But fiction is not as strange as life (so they say)
And misunderstandings are not eloquent
Nor do they create believable and sustainable and longed-for
Love stories.

Thousands like her have accounts accrued (more or less)
From writing misunderstandings with conflicts resolved before the
Final chapter and although the male protagonists do not think (or act!)
Like real men --and the heroines are too real -- we call them romantic
Love stories.

I think our love story is more realistic (it isn't fiction) and
Romantic because misunderstandings like ones on paper are
Blatantly solvable with simple words and we (much wiser) spend our
Time, over, and over, willfully loving and willfully forgiving
Only occasionally do we allow conflict; I concede we fumble about and must
Willfully forgive and (yes, truth) we
Willfully... misunderstand...
And now I realize Jane was right (one of the few?) about
Love stories.

I Breathe, I Joy

(*1998)

I breathe in the words you speak to my heart
And ignore all the possible flaws
While you, in your confidence, carry the sense
Of what each existence may cause.

I dance with your spirit --the way I have dreamed
I'd dance forever; today!
Your leading stirs something Beauty has named
Which carries me swiftly away.

I sing every glance your eyes send to me
A song from inside my soul.
The warmth of my voice soothes every sound --
Your music is all that I know.

I joy in the strength of all that you are
To me, my life, and my dreams.
Giving me courage to love my own self
So your Love is all I may need.

I wrote this as a gift for my husband while we were dating; I happened to give it to him just an hour before he proposed.

Give Me a Fragment

About the Author

Cheryl Seely Savage was born to Canadian parents and raised in southeastern Idaho. She has a Bachelor's degree in Family Studies, eight children, and is married to her favorite person. When she isn't writing poetry, she is teaching piano lessons, reading novels, ignoring the laundry, planning dream vacations, romanticizing, managing chaos, conquering depression, and practicing her faith. Cheryl and her family currently reside in the Flint Hills of Kansas.

Made in the USA
Monee, IL
05 December 2020